PLUVIAL GARDENS

KYLE KNAPP

Copyright © 2012-2013 by Kyle Knapp

All Rights Reserved. No part of this book may be reproduced in any form or by any means without the prior written consent of the publisher, except where permitted by law.

Cover image from iStock (www.istockphoto.com); Design by dMix. Photo of snowy woods and pond taken by Kyle Knapp.

ISBN: 978-0-9833775-9-7

BEAT to a PULP
PO Box 173
Freeville, New York 13068

Email: btapzine@beattoapulp.com
Visit us at www.beattoapulp.com

Contents

Violets	1
The Gray Fenland	2
Ashes of Stone	3
Cursive, Gray Forests	4
An Island	5
Dead Glass	6
The Philter of Red Night	7
Phyrgia	8
The Sanicles of the Cicerone	9
Falling Along the Golden Strath	10
A Statue of Galatea	11
Delores Haze	12
Pluvial Gardens	14
The Pond	16
The Torn Neck of Christ	18
Time	19
Travel	20
Waterfall	22
Laura Palmer	23
The Drowning	24
Cass	25
The Infinite Arcades of Mysterious Seasons	26
In the Eld of Mind, and the Memory of Storms	27
When I'm Old, and the Sun Has Gone Away Again	29

Dedicated to Daniel Jeffery for a friendship I will always remember and to my mother for her steadfast devotion and support.

Violets

She sang in moist whispers
As her pale lips bled
Dripping to the violet branches
Of her glowing violet bed.

I buried my hands in the deep floral frost
That rumored her eyes, spring violets and gray
And I remembered the gardens I walked with her
And the violet fog of starlit clouds
And I remember where I fell against the street
As she died on a dark summer's day.

A Gray Fenland

Digital gray wasps of lightning
Who web the ferrule island fen,
What threat is your answer?
Will you wrap your gentle features
Around the vague lanterns of your courtyard,
Your cerulean stairway of waterfalls,
And the mint carriages that bridge the dark canopy of your
    braided forests?

Will you rip apart your shallow waters,
So your organs can dive into the radiance of forever?
Will you drag these mirrors of rotted fence into your bursting
    green heart
And burn together the walls of the sea?

Ashes of Stone

Wet daisies in the marrows of a tavern wall
Are swallowed by the shore of the lake,
  It burns to the ground on a summer morning.

Caged sea monsters are torn from the pier and ashed in the
    storm,
  White petals of withered stone fall
All around us, like the moon shattering,
A pretended season—
Or a ceremony that the gods perform
To dance in the white flowers,
   Or fall in the pluvial black bloom, or blossom,
(Of the coming storm).

Cursive, Gray Forests

A shade of sea-gold lamplight,
    Fallen to roses
Against the vast autumn-colored cloud lines
        Of cursive, grayed forests.

Where I thought of her eyes,
    Flowering and hollowed
        By brilliant meridian petals,
Where we collapsed
In the pale brook.

(Will you remember me?
    Because I don't think that I can.)

An Island

Tomorrow is borrowed
 From an insular tempest
  On a dying planet.

The mind is a floral ambage
 Of terse vines
  That rapture its falling shore.

November is dripping from the blistered selenian coral,
Hail covers our window
And the fences puncture a hill of clouds
Creasing its wet bark
Framing all of the colors of autumn forever.

Dead Glass

Dead glass crawls across our hands
A scream runs by laughing
A crow's face falls into a pond
And her shadow shakes across the ceiling.

The Philter of Red Night

An argent rain fell
Like a dark frozen wine
Spilled from coruscate eyes.

Sands collapse through her wrinkled teeth
Their endless blinking mural haunting,
I thought of the elation wanton of her wrists
And to offer Morpheus the philter of red night.

And then maybe someday, we'll wake up together
In the sun
In a Scottish heather,
Maybe we won't remember
And I'll love her again forever.

Phrygia

Warm crying dream
Of women damp in evening clouds
"Phrygia; Land of Roses"
Where Aeolus is king
That is where they took her
On a paper ship.

THE SANICLES OF THE CICERONE

As she enters the garden
Amethyst icicles enshroud the glittering trellis
And shatter the window with an urgent embrace.

I watched as the daylight constructs around her the columns
    of the ancient solarium
The columns glow in the blue sun
Like a beautiful selenian mystery falling to earth.

Deep in the forest, cerulean phantoms walk across the
    fountains
And on the quay circle their thousand resplendent shadows.

When we reached the gates we were instructed
By the sanicles of the cicerone
To drink the wet amber from his ghost
And walk with him across the water.

Falling Along the Golden Strath

At night the women
Clad in white,
The fey youth of forgotten arbors,
 Wander through the soft floral halls
Of faraway isles,
 Dripping from the fingers of the trees.
Reflecting in the fog,
On the floor of the orchard
 She appears
 A smile in the crimson and marble.
He sees her sometimes, every few years again—
Wandering—
In the sparkling mists of the vale
That light the shores of the cemetery.

So again tonight, as on any other,
 He will make a wish upon a shadow.
And pray to the doves of another time and light
That borrowed the eyes of the children of his village,
To reward their death with the vision of flight
And tonight the women of the orchard will pass through his
     sleep
And tomorrow a wet corpse will hang from the crimson
     cloudbanks
     In the fields of the dreaming god
Where they will live on forever in the open skies.

A Statue of Galatea

A statue of Galatea,
Is Rotting against an forgotten gate
As Neptune dances the searchlights.

Opaque is the shale limb in the shadows
Rotted by the dawn tide
And as if in another life.

The angelic lambent echoes
Of archaic reptilian communion
Along the corners of every column
Mark the slow crushing gate
Of stone against the lake.

Hollow Jovian smiles
From the faceless crowd
Of the blood-painted solar amphitheater
Pour down from above,
Delighted,
Every coronet bowed,
And "lowered into the horizon"—again.

A cascade of dark gray,
 Ocean walls of electric rain
Conceal the fragile cerement within the falling tide
And carry the thrashing edifice
Far away into the troubled waters
And into the unconscious
Of the distant mortal strife.

Delores Haze

Lovely lariat, Lola.
Long
And lithe.
Bloody your lips
Stain garnet your hips
Sow stars to your eyes
"My love, my life, my child, my bride."
---*(for Nabokov)*

Pluvial Gardens

As a cursive glass vapor
Florid are the organs of the river
In the soft, immortal chorus of winter
In the glowing sleep of the black roses,
    Twisted in the arms of an opaline branch
        Pulsing with the warm blood of the evening
  clouds
(Our last memory of earth).

"I wait to take them inside the lantern"
Into the mind of summer's curtain
Where the seas,
 Suspended,
Decaying in the light
Are lowered into the horizon
A shapeless pupil of burning white
Reflecting in the chords of smoke
Taken from its nest the eye
Taken into the orchard at night
A fence is dragged along her face
Leaving a coruscate red eclipse of heather
In the infinite colloseum of silver bowers
(The living archives of the asylum).

Revolving blue petals
Dim the soft silent rotting rooms.

Where we were forbidden to walk on the new walls—
They were wet with silvered fissures
 And effaced by the foil of the cypress vine—

"The Ageless Labyrinth of the Sun," someone laughed at the
    guide.
A glass spine, dilated by fluorescent mirrors
 Explodes at the end of the hall, shattering,
 Lifted by a windspell of paper-gray lightning
An arbor of thornapple burns bright in the soft, silent wake
And the chandelier takes another hue.
"Woah," someone laughed, as the end of the gallery passed
And everyone left the museum,
  As I stepped with the blinded women, hand in hand to the
    wooden terrace
    The clouds crawled from the waste like shimmering
    roses,
          And the heather blushed in the snow, pale
carmine to a pulse of opal.

I told her of the pluvial gardens
Of the terse white gloam
Of the rotting billows of ashen snow
That blow the silken frost of hemlock so cold
Swathed in a bower of magenta and stone.

The Pond

The children enter a mirror of pale obsidian glass
Against the angelic bough of knotted maple and pine, it
    rested in the grass
Held far from the dark floor of the thick red moonlit tree line
The stained contracted surface shimmers, blinking against
    the light thrice.

In the deep lyrical winter forest
Of the stark, endless evening coppice
Where the clouds begin each year to pour
 From the earth like fountains of floral magenta.

In the bending lambent of summer
In the bending halls of a marble tower
On the burning cornice of the last isle
A boy appears
 So many miles
 Into the cold black blear
Of the harsh and blackest hour
 Of the furrowed skyline.

And the phantom child, his crippled sister
Sits underwater
Smoking dreams
From the roots of the pond.

In the village, deluged
Reds are snow, warm and living
The mortals threaten with raging fires
As the entire sky begins to drain
Into the womb

Of a dead bird
And the children are home
-To this world no longer.

The Torn Neck of Christ

Sinuous furrows of foliage black
The torn neck of Christ
Filled with sand,
And lollipop red
Knotted with spiders,
A well of rainbow blood
Ashen, his pallor
The rags that hang from the summer shrine
Where hatched the soul of a dead god.

TIME

Sable street
In the window white
 A shadow of blue
Crawls from the trees
Through the gate
Dragging the frayed sconce
(The umbilical cord)
Through the night.

Travel

A chlorine-green dream cloud of dust
Covers a stone floor of soft pale velvet hair
 Raked politely into a puddle of stale plastic strawberry
    canvas
On the ground, alone, I think I am.

The sun was the limit of his boozy glance, or gaze
Crayola red pine drifts across the snow
Alcohol rotted farina—drowned
All over my leg, all over the gloves.

There is a car running, to himself prostrate
To the furled limbs neighbor
With damp braces bitten into a crumpled tire
And lights replaced by broken columns of the garage gate.

After wallowing in madness and terror
I am warmed and long to wonder,
And know the auspice
 Of forever,
Never knowing
 The arrogance to license myself as a driver, or motorist,
And I know the memory of arriving home late by the grace
    of a neighbor.

I know that I'll never drive embittered a besotted mad-man
Through the glorious labyrinthine hallways of the American
    Landscape,
And I'll never drag the neighbor's child across the train
    tracks again
Folding with the eyes

Through the whorl of snowfall
Forever biting at the tires
Absent a jaw, drained of spit
 And tried by nauseous abrasion.

   But to not have known the hands of engorged metallic
      silken branches
 Falling through the liquid night of summer's curtain!
To watch in the mirror your eyes
Become an orchard of halogen fireflies
Because so young I'd resigned to the languid lamentations of
      experiences—vicarial
And abandoned myself to the reckless husk of gems
 In the cool verdure of scintillating youth.

WATERFALL

The dripping blond blushing iris of the waterfall,
Wonders
And wanders,
Wearing her cold, worn willow-vair lashes
 Against the falling stone.

Laura Palmer

Pull the body through the plastic
And the carmine ghost
Through the pale sand.

How many times can I inure (I wonder)
This wretched cascade of inhuman horror?

Can I fall to floor of the unfurling—florescent
    antechamber—
And stumble across my blood—lost human spine—
 Through the doors
                    Into the marsh
                          And purge my blood
                                Into the banks
Because now I know her name ...

The Drowning

The cold fronds meadowed
By the dry summer wind
And the frost,
 Colored as wine
 And the cold clouds of the meadow.
Arranged far below
 The ancient swelling vines
Reaching every branch,
Encoiled every flower.

The accosted survivor,
Drying his tears with matches,
 Walks past us
 Staggering by.
He walks into the pond
Leaving the swirling, verdant world
 Far, far behind
And never more will we see again or rumor
Those burnt, yellowing eyes
Fading into the foam.

But all the flowers that were ever alive
Have conspired to the murder.
But will you, they ask,
"Encourage the Wrists of the Witness."

Will you scatter into the disturbance
And forget that you killed her?

Cass

The terse, living-gray tissues of the cloud wall
That are breaking against the light and glass
Unfurl the crystalline catacombs of the banisters
And the aging wreaths of frost
 That tinsel the roseate lanterns.

That they glare against her eyes at last
 As she passes, smiling
An ancient shade of verdigris
Bursting behind every fallen lash.

Writhing on the stones of the shallow pier
Below the searchlights
Dancing
Across the starlit iris of sun-dyed snow
Through the burnished memories of another life
Those memories of the future
That are worth waiting for
 If ever we can.

The Infinite Arcades of Mysterious Seasons

The restless limbs of frozen branches
Re-arrange the infinite arcades
        Of mysterious seasons.

(In the allergy of the After
And after the infinite).

The architects have returned to their garden to recompose the
    tragedy of time;
Is an endless mutation The Accident Of Consciousness?
Is the birth of the gods?
Is time a symptom of sentience
Or the blisters of our father's cage?
Does the moon burn your eyes? she asks.

In the Eld of Mind, and the Memory of Storms

A storm-densed shadow
On the moonlit quay
 Eclipsed each night
 By the falling rain.

He, the shadow, the shade
The echo of the slow endless slumber
 Can feel the glittering whorl
Of the glistening, outer world
And the mind therein
That lies inside
 Of that skeleton encaved
 In the dark wooded ground
From which he stood up slowly, from the sodden earthen
    planks
 Illuminated only
 By the gentle blue snow.

And the mind inside, that therein lies
Is fluctuating in radio-like static punctuations
 With sundry bursts of sudden, forgotten, and longing songs.

The mind is still spinning around the fire
 An incandescence
 Tornado of glass
Contracting and exploding
Another world
That spins around the fire
Waiting to be born again.

When I'm Old, and the Sun Has Gone Away Again

Dolorous ring of vine
And helicoid floral shaw
Admit me to your dour hanging
Spherical—spine—
 Of hollow auburn sorrows.

Let me sit by your ashes
Some day, when I'm old
And the sun has gone away again
And I can truly sleep
By the heel of your crest.

☦

About the Author

Kyle Knapp was born in Cortland, New York in the month of September, 1989. Bored and restricted by the educational system, he left school at the age of sixteen to pursue a degree in sociology at a local college. He worked as an English tutor for the college during the fall and spent his summers tending the flower groves of Willow Glen Cemetery. Kyle began writing and collecting volumes of poetry at the age of fifteen, amassing a large body of work that is ready to share. Kyle lives in New York in a small home beside the riverbank of Fall Creek.

 BEAT to a PULP
PO Box 173
Freeville, New York 13068

Email: btapzine@beattoapulp.com
Visit us at www.beattoapulp.com

www.ingramcontent.com/pod-product-compliance
Lightning Source LLC
Chambersburg PA
CBHW020024050426
42450CB00005B/638